SCHOLASTIC
News
Nonfiction Readers®

Our Earth
Making Less Trash

by Peggy Hock

Children's Press®
An Imprint of Scholastic Inc.
New York Toronto London Auckland Sydney
Mexico City New Delhi Hong Kong
Danbury, Connecticut

These content vocabulary word builders are for grades 1–2.

Content Adviser: Zoe Chafe, Research Associate, Worldwatch Institute, Washington, DC

Reading Consultant: Cecilia Minden-Cupp, PhD, Early Literacy Consultant and Author, Chapel Hill, North Carolina

Photographs © 2009: Alamy Images: 23 bottom right (Mark Boulton), 15 (Phil Degginger), 13 (Epicscotland.com), back cover, 4 bottom left, 9 (David R. Frazier Photolibrary, Inc.), 2, 17 (Angela Hampton Picture Library), 5 bottom left, 16 (Thorsten Indra), 11 main (PhotoAlto); AP Images/Kevork Djansezian: 23 top left; Courtesy of Cagoule Fleece: 23 bottom left; Corbis Images/Tatiana Markow/Sygma: 21 center; Getty Images: 4 top, 8 (Martin Bernetti), 1, 5 top left, 7 (James Hardy); Masterfile: cover; PhotoEdit: 5 bottom right, 11 inset (Mary Kate Denny), 20 bottom, 20 top, 21 bottom, 21 top (Tony Freeman), 4 bottom right, 12, 19 (David Young-Wolff); Play Mart, Inc./Tabitha Beach: 23 top right (Mega Play System - Jordan); ShutterStock, Inc./Tyler Olsen: 5 top right, 14.

Book Design: Simonsays Design!
Book Production: The Design Lab

Library of Congress Cataloging-in-Publication Data
Hock, Peggy, 1948–
Our Earth : making less trash / By Peggy Hock.
   p. cm.—(Scholastic news nonfiction readers)
Includes bibliographical references and index.
ISBN-13: 978-0-531-13834-2 (lib. bdg.) 978-0-531-20434-4 (pbk.)
ISBN-10: 0-531-13834-8 (lib. bdg.) 0-531-20434-0 (pbk.)
1. Recycling (Waste, etc.)—Juvenile literature. I. Title. II. Series.
TD794.5.H63 2008
640—dc22   2007051903

CONTENTS

WORD HUNT

Look for these words as you read. They will be in **bold**.

air pollution
(ayr puh-**loo**-shuhn)

landfill
(**land**-fill)

packaging
(**pa**-kuhj-ing)

garbage trucks
(**gar**-bij truhks)

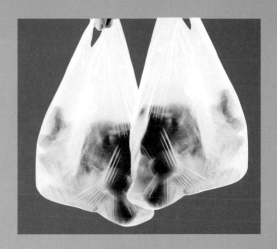

grocery bags
(**grohs**-ree bagz)

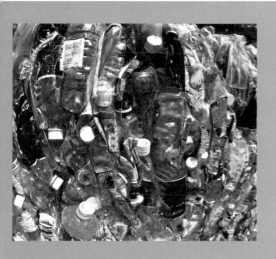

plastic
(**plas**-tik)

recycle
(ree-**sye**-kuhl)

How Much Garbage?

How much goes into your trash can each day?

Most Americans throw away more than 4 pounds (2 kilograms) of trash each day.

Together, Americans fill thousands of **garbage trucks** every day!

Garbage trucks help keep our cities clean. But where does all that garbage go?

Most garbage is taken to a huge dump called a **landfill**.

Landfills use up a lot of land.

Some cities burn their garbage instead.

That saves space, but it can cause **air pollution**.

air pollution

When this landfill is full, the people who live nearby will need a new place to dump their trash.

Getting rid of trash is a problem.

One way to solve that problem is to make less trash.

Everyone can do this by using three rules called the three Rs.

What are the three Rs? They are **R**educe, **R**euse, and **Recycle**.

How can you cut down on the amount of garbage you throw out?

recycle

The first R stands for **R**educe. Reduce means to use less.

One way to use less is to buy only what you need.

Try to buy things without a lot of **packaging**. Empty packages take up a lot of landfill space.

packaging

Many packages will be thrown away after this meal. How could you pack a trash-free lunch?

The second R is for **R**euse. That means to use things again instead of throwing them away.

You can reuse **grocery bags**. You can also reuse paper by writing on the back.

grocery bags

What can you do with toys or clothes you don't need anymore? Give them away, or have a garage sale.

The last R stands for **R**ecycle.

To recycle means to make new things from old things.

Paper, glass, and **plastic** take up most of the space in landfills.

They can be recycled into new products instead.

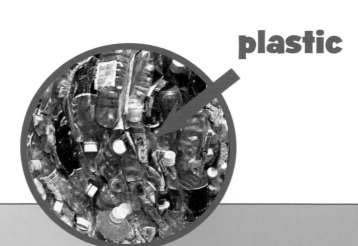

plastic

Reducing, reusing, and recycling can keep trash out of landfills.

That is one way to help keep our world healthy.

Think of ways you can use the three Rs.

You may be able to help the planet, and have some fun, too!

You can make art while you recycle and reuse!

Making New Paper from Old

1

Old newspaper is shredded.

2

Water and chemicals clean the paper. The ink comes off.

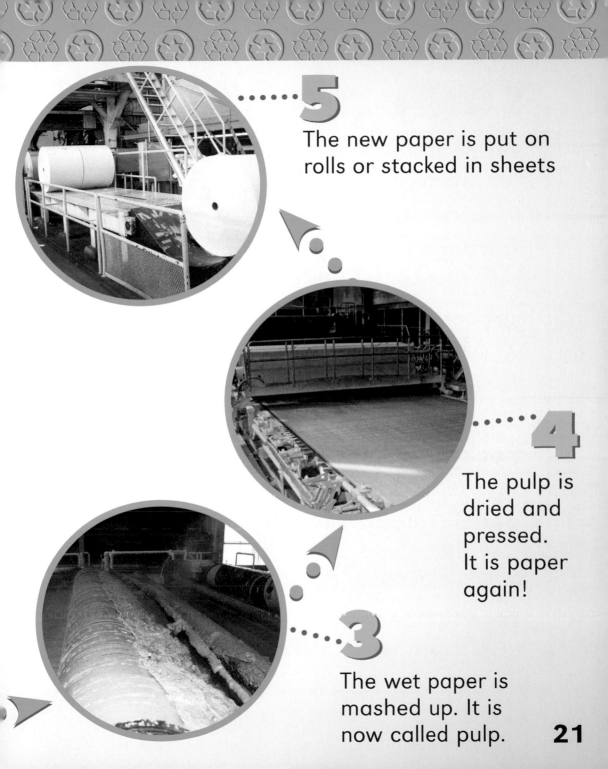

5

The new paper is put on rolls or stacked in sheets

4

The pulp is dried and pressed. It is paper again!

3

The wet paper is mashed up. It is now called pulp.

YOUR NEW WORDS

air pollution (ayr puh-**loo**-shuhn) harmful materials that make the air dirty and unhealthy to breathe

garbage trucks (**gar**-bij truhks) vehicles that collect trash

grocery bags (**grohs**-ree bagz) bags used to carry food home from a store

landfill (**land**-fill) an area where garbage is safely dumped and buried

packaging (**pa**-kuhj-ing) the box or wrapping that covers the things you buy

plastic (**plas**-tik) a human-made material that is strong and light; plastic can be molded into many different shapes

recycle (ree-**sye**-kuhl) to make old plastic, paper, glass, and metal into new objects

W ̶ ̶ ̶
RECYCLED PLASTIC

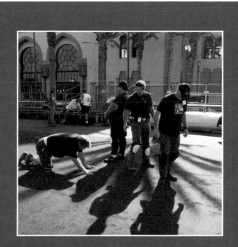

Carpets

Playground equipment

Hats

Picnic tables

INDEX

FIND OUT MORE

Book:

Pohl, Kathleen. *What Happens at a Recycling Center?* Milwaukee, WI: Weekly Reader Early Learning Library, 2007.

Website:

Act Green—Scholastic.com
http://www.scholastic.com/actgreen/

MEET THE AUTHOR

Peggy Hock lives near San Francisco, California. She likes to go backpacking in the mountains of the Sierra Nevada with her husband and two grown children. She used both sides of the paper to write this book.